Message to Parents

Congratulations on your child's participation in the American Red Cross Swimming and Water Safety program. This booklet is an important part of your child's swimming experience. We encourage you and your child to read this booklet together during this session. It includes—

- A story line that supports and reinforces what your child is learning.
- Achievement cards that indicate your child's progress toward passing Red Cross Preschool Aquatics Level 3 and Learn-to-Swim Levels 2 and 3. Your child's instructor will complete the appropriate achievement card at the end of each session.
- Activities to help you practice with your child.
- Tips for safe diving to help keep you and your family safe from injuries to the head, neck and back.
- A chart that provides an overview of Red Cross Preschool Aquatics and Learn-to-Swim courses.

You can play a role in helping your child learn to swim! You can help by—

- Providing for your child's safety around water at all times.
- Maintaining enthusiasm and a positive attitude about learning to swim.
- Ensuring that your child attends each swim lesson.
- Discussing and applying water safety rules.
- Practicing the fundamental skills your child is learning in class.

Page 14 suggests activities to do with your child that reinforce what he or she is learning. At these levels, your child has basic aquatic skills, but there must always be active adult supervision whenever your child is in the water.

Encourage your child to show you the skills he or she is learning in class. Your interest and enthusiasm for the progress your child is achieving is a great motivator! You can use the achievement cards in this booklet as a prompt to remind your child and describe the skills if he or she has difficulty remembering. Also, talk with your child's instructor. The instructor can explain specific activities or drills you can use to help with problem areas.

It is important to know that your child is learning headfirst entries now. Your child must know the rules of safe diving and safe areas in which to dive.

It cannot be overemphasized that participation in any swim lesson program will not "drownproof" your child. It is only the first step in developing your child's water safety and swimming skills. Year-round practice, regular exposure to water and positive encouragement are the tools needed for developing your child's comfort level in water and improving his or her swimming skills.

The Red Cross strongly recommends that a swimmer engage in water activities only where there is active adult supervision. Continue your child's swimming and water safety education by progressing through all the levels of Red Cross Learn-to-Swim.

Contact your local Red Cross chapter for further information.

Waddles In The Deep

This book belongs to _____

"Are you ready for swim lessons, Waddles?" asked Sophie Dog excitedly.

"I sure am!" answered Waddles. "I can't wait to learn to jump into deep water!"

Mr. Casey Condor, the American Red Cross instructor, greeted Waddles, Sophie and the rest of the class.

"My name is Mr. Casey. Let's talk about some of the things you'll be learning. You'll learn how to jump and dive into the pool. You'll also start to learn about the front crawl and the elementary backstroke."

Everyone's eyes got big with excitement. "Oooh! Ahh," they said.

3

"Let's review some of the water safety rules we've already learned," said Mr. Casey. "Who can remember a rule?" Mr. Casey asked the class.

Waddles raised his hand and said, "Swim with a Buddy in a Supervised Area."

"That's right! Only go swimming when there is an adult who knows you are going to swim and is watching you," said Mr. Casey. "What's another rule?"

"Be Cool, Follow the Rule!" said Hatch Alligator proudly.

"Absolutely!" said Mr. Casey. "Another rule is: Think So You Don't Sink. How many of you have seen someone get into trouble in the water?"

Eddie Elephant raised his hand and said, "My cousin once got a cramp in her leg while she was swimming."

"That's a good example," said Mr. Casey. "If you get into trouble in the water, always stay calm. When Eddie's cousin got a leg cramp, she should have relaxed and rubbed her cramped muscle."

4

"Mr. Casey, what if I see someone in trouble in the water?" asked Waddles.

"Ah, now that's another rule: Reach or Throw, Don't Go. To be safe, either reach out from the side of the pool or throw a rope, ball, large branch or anything that floats. Then get help. Remember, do not try to get in the water and rescue someone by yourself!" said Mr. Casey.

"Let's practice."

Being in the water and learning new strokes was Waddles' favorite part of swim lessons. Mr. Casey taught them strokes to swim on their front and back. Waddles was quite proud of his front crawl.

As the students practiced, Mr. Casey helped them get better. They got better and better as they practiced more and more. But sometimes Sophie had some problems making her legs cooperate.

"Now let's get into the deep end of the pool by jumping from the side," said Mr. Casey.

Waddles was a bit nervous. He had never jumped into the deep end. He watched his other classmates jump right in with a splash and swim right back to the side of the pool. "On the count of 3," he thought to himself, "I'll do it."

"1…2…3." Waddles jumped into the pool and made a great big splash!

He came out of the water with a huge smile! "I did it!" Waddles exclaimed.

9 Ft

"You can enter deep water another way—starting with your fingertips, followed by your head and the rest of your body. I'll show you how it looks," said Mr. Casey.

Mr. Casey extended his arms over his head, squeezing his ears tightly, and entered the water with very little splash. He came right back up to the surface of the water to the sounds of children cheering.

"I want to try! I want to try!" everyone chanted. Everyone, that is, except Waddles.

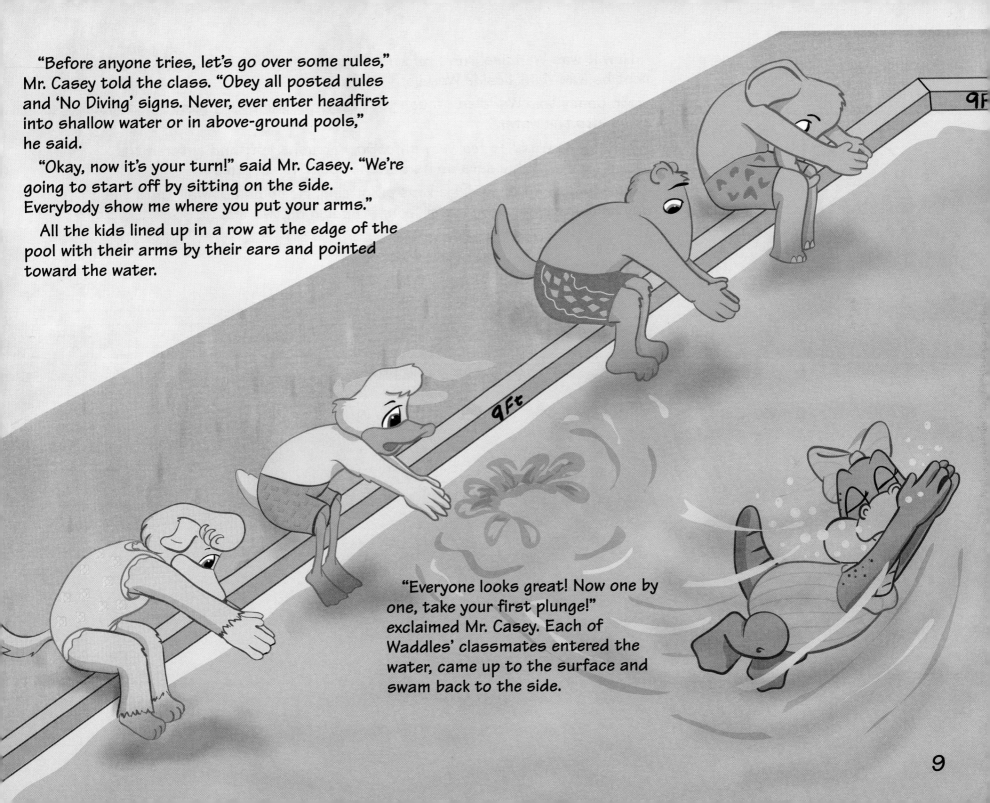

"Before anyone tries, let's go over some rules," Mr. Casey told the class. "Obey all posted rules and 'No Diving' signs. Never, ever enter headfirst into shallow water or in above-ground pools," he said.

"Okay, now it's your turn!" said Mr. Casey. "We're going to start off by sitting on the side. Everybody show me where you put your arms."

All the kids lined up in a row at the edge of the pool with their arms by their ears and pointed toward the water.

"Everyone looks great! Now one by one, take your first plunge!" exclaimed Mr. Casey. Each of Waddles' classmates entered the water, came up to the surface and swam back to the side.

9

Now it was Waddles' turn. He was a bit nervous, but Mr. Casey moved so that he was right beside Waddles.

Mr. Casey told Waddles, "Touch your fingers against my hands and follow them into the water."

This made Waddles feel very safe. So, he pushed off and entered the water, squeezing his ears as hard as he could. It was great!

This was all he needed. He kept practicing. He could not wait until the day he could enter deep water from standing on two feet!

9 Ft

10

On the last day of swim lessons, everyone was very excited. On this day, they were going to show their parents how much they learned.

The students proudly demonstrated the many different things they could do in the water. The parents cheered wildly.

After class was over, Waddles and his mom were leaving the pool. With a happy and proud look, Waddles asked his mom, "When does my next swim lesson start?"

Preschool Aquatics
Level 3
Achievement Card

Instructor:_____ Date:_____

Skills

- ❏ Enter water by jumping in
- ❏ Fully submerging and holding breath, 5 seconds
- ❏ Bobbing, 5 times (in chest-deep water)
- ❏ Front float, 5 seconds
- ❏ Jellyfish float, 5 seconds
- ❏ Tuck float, 5 seconds
- ❏ Recover from a front float or glide to a vertical position
- ❏ Back float, 15 seconds
- ❏ Back glide, 2 body lengths
- ❏ Recover from a back float or glide to a vertical position
- ❏ Change direction of travel while swimming on front or back
- ❏ Treading using arm and leg actions, 15 seconds (in shoulder-deep water)
- ❏ Combined arm and leg actions on front, 5 body lengths
- ❏ Finning arm action on back, 5 body lengths
- ❏ Combined arm and leg actions on back, 5 body lengths

Safety Topics

- ❏ Staying safe around aquatic environments
- ❏ Don't just pack it, wear your jacket
- ❏ Recognizing an emergency
- ❏ How to call for help
- ❏ Too much sun is no fun
- ❏ Look before you leap
- ❏ Think so you don't sink
- ❏ Reach or throw, don't go

Exit Skills Assessment

- ❏ Step from side into chest-deep water, move into a front float for 5 seconds, roll to back, float for 5 seconds then return to a vertical position.
- ❏ Move into a back float for 5 seconds, roll to front then recover to a vertical position.
- ❏ Push off and swim using combined arm and leg actions on front for 5 body lengths, roll to back, float for 15 seconds, roll to front then continue swimming for 5 body lengths. (You can assist the child when taking a breath.)

❏ **I Passed!**

Learn-to-Swim
Level 2
Achievement Card

Instructor:_____

Skills

- ❏ Enter water by stepping or jumping from the side (in shoulder-deep water)
- ❏ Exit water using ladder, steps or side (in chest-deep water)
- ❏ Fully submerging and holding breath, 5 seconds
- ❏ Bobbing, 5 times (in chest-deep water)
- ❏ Opening eyes under water and retrieving submerged objects, 2 times
- ❏ Front float, 5 seconds
- ❏ Jellyfish float, 5 seconds
- ❏ Tuck float, 5 seconds
- ❏ Front glide, 2 body lengths
- ❏ Recover from a front float or glide to a vertical position
- ❏ Back float, 15 seconds
- ❏ Back glide, 2 body lengths
- ❏ Recover from a back float or glide to a vertical position
- ❏ Change direction of travel while swimming on front or back
- ❏ Roll from front to back
- ❏ Roll from back to front
- ❏ Treading using arm and leg actions, 15 seconds
- ❏ Combined arm and leg actions on front, 5 body lengths
- ❏ Finning arm action on back, 5 body lengths

Learn-to-Swim
Level 3

Achievement Card

American Red Cross

Date:_____   Instructor:_____   Date:_____

◻ Combined arm and leg actions on back, 5 body lengths

Safety Topics

◻ Staying safe around aquatic environments

◻ Don't just pack it, wear your jacket

◻ Recognizing an emergency

◻ How to call for help

◻ Too much sun is no fun

◻ Look before you leap

◻ Think so you don't sink

◻ Reach or throw, don't go

Exit Skills Assessment

◻ Step from side into chest-deep water, move into a front float for 5 seconds, roll to back, float for 5 seconds then return to vertical position.

◻ Move into a back float for 5 seconds, roll to front then recover to a vertical position.

◻ Push off and swim using combined arm and leg actions on front for 5 body lengths, roll to back, float for 15 seconds, roll to the front then continue swimming for 5 body lengths. (You can assist the participant when taking a breath.)

Skills

◻ Enter water by jumping from the side

◻ Headfirst entry from the side in a sitting position (in water at least 9-feet deep)

◻ Headfirst entry from the side in a kneeling position (in water at least 9-feet deep)

◻ Bobbing while moving toward safety, 5 times

◻ Rotary breathing, 10 times

◻ Survival float on front, 30 seconds

◻ Back float, 30 seconds

◻ Change from vertical to horizontal position on front

◻ Change from vertical to horizontal position on back

◻ Tread water, 30 seconds

◻ Push off in a streamlined position on front then begin flutter kicking, 3–5 body lengths

◻ Push off in a streamlined position on front then begin dolphin kicking, 3–5 body lengths

◻ Front crawl, 15 yards

◻ Elementary backstroke, 15 yards

◻ Scissors kick, 10 yards

Safety Topics

◻ Reach or throw, don't go

◻ Think twice before going near cold water or ice

◻ Look before you leap

Exit Skills Assessment

◻ Jump into deep water from the side, swim front crawl for 15 yards, maintain position by treading or floating for 30 seconds and swim elementary backstroke for 15 yards.

◻ **I Passed!**

◻ **I Passed!**

Helping Your Child Progress

Safety Tour

Take your child on a guided tour of the swimming area. Explain the rules of the swimming area. Be sure your child knows that the swimming area is off limits unless an adult is present to supervise. Also, be sure to review the diving safety rules that are included in this booklet. Stress to your child where it is safe to dive and be clear about where diving is prohibited.

Entering the Water

Hands Down, Hands Out, Hands Up—Have your child jump from the edge of the pool into deep water. As your child begins to jump, shout out one of the following phrases:

- Hands down: Child enters the water with the hands below the hips
- Hands out: Child enters the water with the hands at shoulder level
- Hands up: Child enters the water with the hands above the head

Submersion and Underwater Exploration

Egg Hunt—Fill different colored plastic eggs with about 10 pennies. It may be necessary to tape the seams. Drop the eggs into different depths of water, depending on your child's ability. Begin in shallow water. As your child gains confidence and skill, drop the eggs into deeper depths. Tell your child that on your command, he or she is to submerge and gather as many eggs in the color that you call out as possible. Repeat until all the eggs are gathered.

Underwater Swimming

Underwater Obstacle Course—Have your child swim through a series of hoops placed under water. As your child improves, increase the distance between the hoops to no more than 3 to 5 body lengths. For safety, do not let your child hyperventilate, and make sure the hoops are placed away from the wall so that your child does not strike it while swimming.

Streamline off the Wall—Place a large Hula-hoop 2 to 3 body lengths away from the wall. Have your child push off the wall and swim through the hoop while maintaining a streamlined position. Repeat using a Hula-hoop of smaller diameter. Repeat the activity, each time using a hoop of smaller diameter, to see how small of a hoop your child can go through without touching the sides.

Gliding

Blasting Off—Have your child pretend to be a rocket ship. Have him or her extend the hands overhead and place a foot on the side of pool. Begin a countdown and on your cue, have your child blast off. To blast off, your child puts the face and arms in the water, the other foot on the side and pushes off. Vary the activity by having your child swim on the front and back and add kicks for the "engine booster."

Kicking

Soft Kick, Hard Kick—Have your child bracket on the wall on the front with the legs extended. When you say "Soft Kick," have your child flutter kick as slow and with as small of a kick as possible. When you say "Hard Kick," have your child flutter kick as hard as possible. Repeat 2 or 3 times. Have your child rotate so he or she is bracketed on one side with the legs extended. Repeat the cycle until your child rotates to the front, the other side and then back to the front again. As your child's confidence and ability improves, he or she can use a kickboard with this drill.

Combined Skills

Talking to the Fish—Using a kickboard, have your child put the face in the water and use a kick of his or her choice. With the face in the water, have your child pretend to be talking to the fish. The child talks to the fish by exhaling and blowing bubbles. The child listens to the fish by turning the face to the side so the ear is in the water.

Simon Says—Tell your child that you are going to call out skills, such as treading water or front crawl. Explain that if you say the words, "Simon Says," he or she should do the skills that you say. Explain that if you do not say the words, "Simon Says," he or she should not move. Consult the achievement card for skills.

Be Water Smart

Learn About Diving Safety

A headfirst entry into shallow water is the leading cause of head, neck and back injuries in the water. The following guidelines are recommended for safe diving:

- Learn how to dive safely from a qualified instructor.
- In a headfirst entry, extend the arms with your elbows locked alongside the head. Keep your hands together with thumbs touching (or interlocked) and palms facing toward the water. Keeping the arms, wrists and fingers in line with the head helps control the angle of entry. This reduces the impact of the water on top of the head and helps protect from injury. A diver's body should be tensed and straight from the hands to the pointed toes.
- Follow safety rules at all times—never make exceptions.
- Do not wear earplugs; pressure changes make them dangerous.
- Obey "No Diving" signs. They are there for safety.
- Be sure of water depth and ensure that the water is free from obstructions. The first time in the water, ease in or walk in; do not jump or dive.
- Never dive into an above-ground pool, the shallow end of any in-ground pool or at a beach.
- Never dive into cloudy or murky water where you cannot see the bottom or what is below the surface.
- In open water, always check first for objects under the surface, such as logs, stumps, boulders and pilings.
- Check the shape of the pool bottom to be sure the diving area is large enough and deep enough for the intended dive.
- The presence of a diving board does not necessarily mean it is safe to dive. Pools at homes, motels and hotels might not be safe for diving.
- When diving from a deck, be sure the water is at least 9-feet deep and the area of entry is free of obstructions (such as lane lines and kickboards) for at least 4 feet on both sides. For dives from a 1-meter diving board, the water should be at least 11-feet, 6-inches deep and there should be 10 feet of clearance on both sides.
- Dive only off the end of a diving board. Diving off the side of a diving board might result in striking the side of the pool or entering water that is not deep enough.
- Do not bounce more than once on the end of a diving board in order to avoid missing the edge or slipping off the diving board.
- Do not run on a diving board or attempt to dive a long way through the air. The water might not be deep enough at the point of entry.
- Do not dive from a height greater than 1 meter unless trained in elevated entry.
- Swim away from the diving board after entering the water. Do not be a hazard for the next diver.

Learn About Life Jackets

- Anyone should have and know how to wear a life jacket if they are going to be in, on or around water.
- Even good swimmers should wear a life jacket when boating or water skiing or if there is any chance of accidentally falling or being thrown into the water.
- Although you should always wear your life jacket, it is even more important when the water temperature is cold.
- The U.S. Coast Guard has arranged personal flotation devices into five types. The four wearable types may have permanent flotation or may be inflatable.
  - Type I (offshore life jackets): They turn most unconscious wearers in the water from a face-down position to a vertical or slightly tipped-back position.
  - Type II (near shore): They may help turn an unconscious person in the water from a face-down position to a vertical or slightly tipped-back position. Type II life jackets have less buoyancy than type I life jackets but are more comfortable to wear.
  - Type III (flotation aids): These "float coats" or vests may keep a conscious person in a vertical or slightly tipped-back position. Type III is more comfortable for active water sports than types I and II.
  - Type IV (throwable devices): Flotation devices, such as a buoyant cushion or the ring buoy, are not worn but can be thrown to a person in an emergency. A buoyant cushion may be used as a seat cushion. These devices do not take the place of wearing a life jacket.
  - Type V (restricted-use life jacket): These special purpose devices are approved for specific activities, such as commercial whitewater rafting and riding personal watercraft, where other types of life jackets would be too constrictive or when more protection is necessary.
- When choosing a life jacket—
  - Make sure it is the right type for the right activity.
  - Make sure it is U.S. Coast Guard approved.
  - Make sure it fits the intended user. Check the stamp on the life jacket for weight limits.
  - Make sure it is in good condition. Check buckles and straps for proper function. Discard any life jacket with torn fabric or loose straps.
  - Practice putting it on in water and swimming with it on. When you practice, have a companion with you who can help you if you have difficulty.

What Not to Use

Inflatable toys, such as water wings, swim rings and other flotation devices, are not substitutes for U.S. Coast Guard-approved life jackets or adult supervision. Swimmers may go beyond their ability and fall off, which may lead to a drowning situation. Some inflatable materials deteriorate in the sun and on rough pool surfaces which may lead to deflation and leaks.